Scoliosis

Dr. Alvin Silverstein,

Virginia Silverstein, and

Laura Silverstein Nunn

My Health

Franklin Watts

A Division of Scholastic Inc.

New York • Toronto • London • Auckland • Sydney

Mexico City • New Delhi • Hong Kong

Photographs © 2002: Bertil Holmberg: 32; Corbis Images: 14 (Lester V. Bergman), 18 (Kevin Cozad/O'Brien Productions), 6 (Jennie Woodcock/Reflections Photolibrary); Custom Medical Stock Photo: 8, 11, 23, 37; Photo Researchers, NY: 21 (CC Studio/SPL), 9 (Jim Dowdalls/SS), 28 (Aaron Haupt), 20 (Dr. P. Marazzi/SPL), 4 (Doug Martin), 12 (Hans-Ulrich Osterwalder/SPL), 15, 25 (Princess Margaret Rose Orthopaedic Hospital/SPL); PhotoEdit: 27 (Bill Bachmann), 34 (Cindy Charles), 17 (Tony Freeman), 36 (Bonnie Kamin); Rigoberto Quinteros: 7; Spinal Technology: 30; Visuals Unlimited/SIU: 19, 35.

Cartoons by Rick Stromoski

Library of Congress Cataloging-in-Publication Data

Silverstein, Alvin.
  Scoliosis / by Alvin Silverstein, Virginia Silverstein, and Laura Silverstein Nunn.
     p. cm.
Summary: Discusses the medical condition known as scoliosis, its detection and treatment, and how to live with it.
Includes bibliographical references and index.
  ISBN 0-531-12046-5 (lib. bdg.)   0-531-16639-2 (pbk.)
  1. Scoliosis—Juvenile literature. [1. Scoliosis.] I. Silverstein, Virginia B. II. Nunn, Laura Silverstein. III. Title.
  RD771.S3 S56 2002
  616.7'3—dc21

               2002007389

Contents

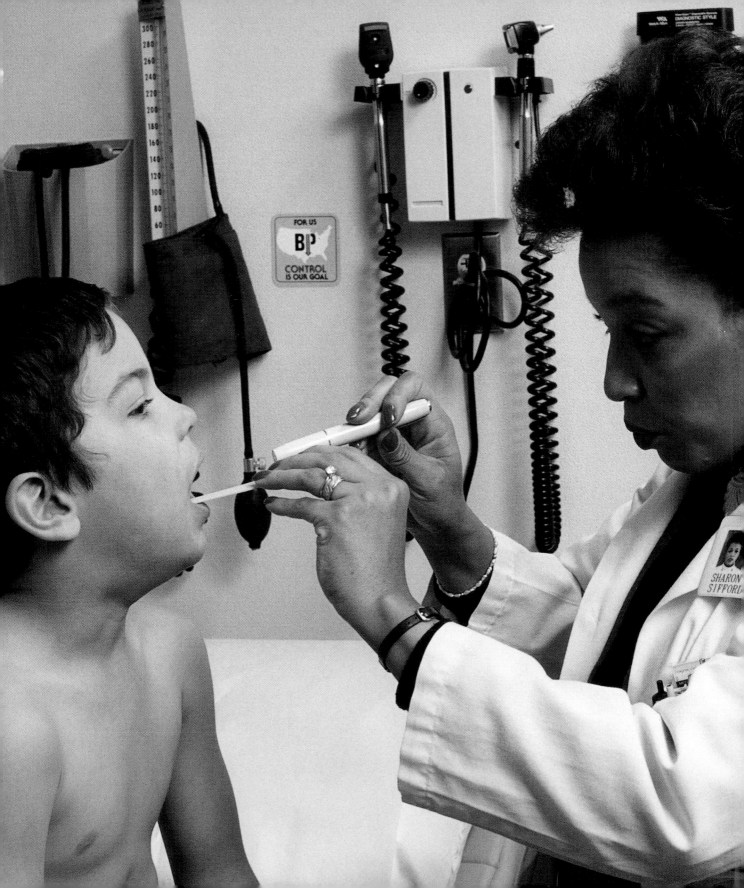

A Curvy Condition

Have you ever gone to the doctor when you felt fine? Doctors encourage kids to get routine check-ups even if they feel okay, just to make sure everything is working normally. You're probably familiar with the routine. You may have to open your mouth and say "Ahhh..." so the doctor can look at your throat. He or she may shine a little flashlight in each of your eyes and put an instrument in each of your ears to make sure they look okay. The doctor may also use a little hammer to tap against your knees to check your reflexes.

The doctor might even ask you to bend over and touch your toes—not to find out if you can reach your feet, but to get a look at your backbone, or **spine**. This is to check for a condition called **scoliosis**, in which the spine curves from

Did You Know...

Scoliosis is a condition that develops while a child is growing. You can't catch it from someone who has it.

◀ **Most children get regular check-ups at least once a year.**

5

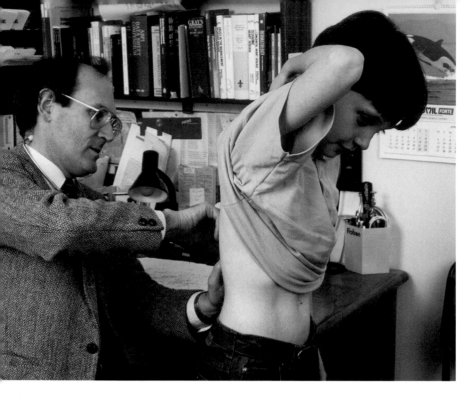

side to side. In fact, the term *scoliosis* comes from a Greek word that means "crooked-ness" or "curve."

It is very important to spot scoliosis early, while the body is still growing. If this condi-tion is not treated, it may get worse. It can cause serious problems in your chest and back. Scoliosis can affect the way you sit, walk, and even breathe. That is why routine check-ups of children and teens usually include checking for scoliosis.

In many cases, scoliosis can be treated successfully with special back braces. They hold the spine in place and keep the curve from getting worse. If the curve is too great, though, an operation may be needed to straighten it out.

Doctors are not sure what causes scoliosis, but it is easier to treat if it is spotted early. The more you and your family learn about this condition, the better chance you have of spotting it before it gets serious.

The Spine

When people talk about the backbone or spine, it sounds like they are describing a long, solid bone. But if that were true, you wouldn't be able to bend easily to pick up an object or twist your body to move. The spine is actually made up of separate bones called **vertebrae**.

If you bend forward and feel along the middle of your back, you can feel little bumps running down in a straight line starting at your neck. These little bumps are back parts of the vertebrae. You may have as many as thirty-three, but an adult has only twenty-six vertebrae. This is because some of the vertebrae grow together as you get older.

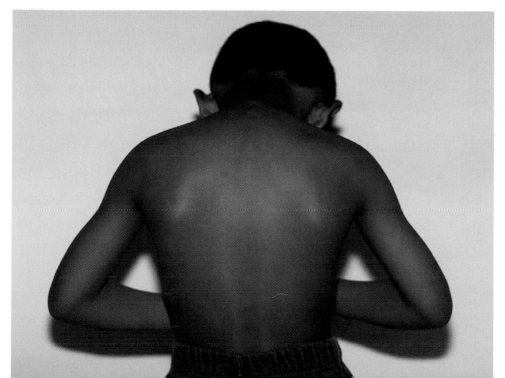

The little bumps that run down your spine mark the individual bones called vertebrae.

The vertebrae are stacked, each on top of the next, to form the spine. The spine goes from your neck down to your rear end. The individual bones fit together in **joints** that allow for some movement. The joints in your spine do not permit as much movement as those in your knees or fingers, but you can bend forward and turn in any direction.

Ligaments and muscles (shown on the right) are attached to the vertebrae.

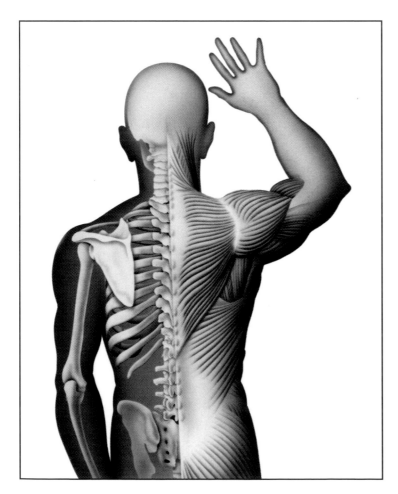

Each vertebra is round in the front and has bony knobs on the sides and back. It is one of these bony knobs from each vertebra that you feel when you run your fingers down your back. **Ligaments** and **muscles** are attached to the knobs. Ligaments are strong straps that hold the bones together, but at the same time let them bend easily so you can move, sit, and stand. The vertebrae are also supported by many muscles, which help the spine to move. The muscles of the back, neck, and shoulders also work to keep the spine lined up and straight.

Between each of the vertebrae is a cushion of tough, rubbery **cartilage**, similar to the gristle you find at the end of chicken bones. These cushions, called **disks**, are your natural shock absorbers. They help to absorb the bumps and jolts every time you walk, jump, or bend.

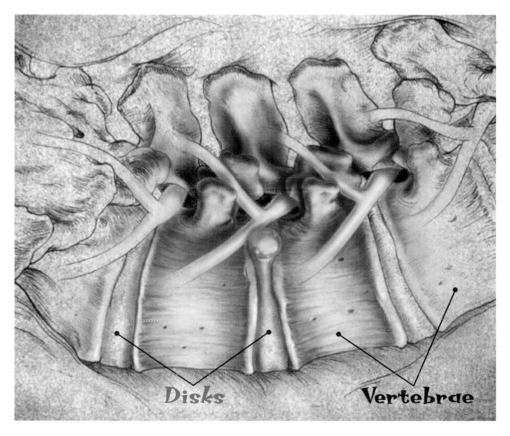

The cushions of cartilage between vertebrae are called disks.

Disks

Vertebrae

You're Shrinking!

When you go to bed at night, you may be as much as half an inch shorter than when you got up in the morning. That's because all your daily activities pound on the rubbery disks between the vertebrae. The disks make up about 25% of the spine's entire length. As the day goes by, the disks get squashed. While you sleep, the disks recover their cushiony thickness. But as you get older, they will lose some of their ability to recover. So adults actually get a little shorter as they age.

Doctors divide the spine into three main groups of vertebrae. The first is the **cervical vertebrae**, which include the top seven bones of the spine. These vertebrae support the neck and the skull. Without them, your head would droop like a wilted flower.

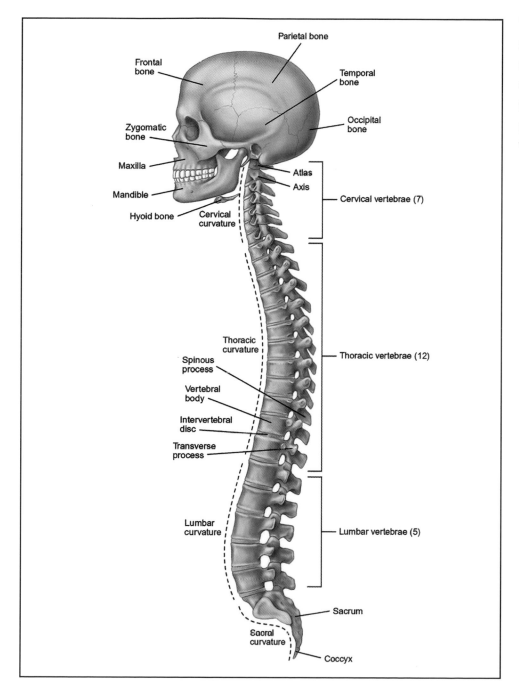

Parietal bone

Frontal bone

Temporal bone

Zygomatic bone

Occipital bone

Maxilla

Mandible

Atlas

Axis

Hyoid bone

Cervical curvature

Cervical vertebrae (7)

Thoracic curvature

Spinous process

Vertebral body

Intervertebral disc

Transverse process

Thoracic vertebrae (12)

Lumbar curvature

Lumbar vertebrae (5)

Sacrum

Sacral curvature

Coccyx

This diagram shows how medical experts divide the spine into groups of vertebrae.

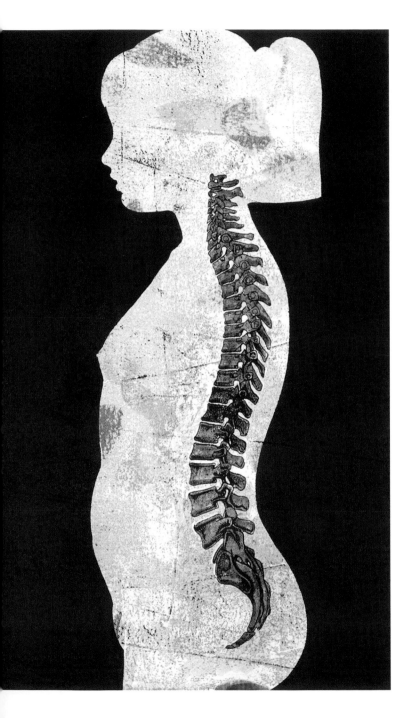

After the cervical vertebrae is the next group, the twelve **thoracic vertebrae** in the chest area. They are attached to the ribs. These are the bones that give you support when you lean against the back of a chair. Each thoracic vertebra is larger than the one above it.

The back muscles are supported by the next five vertebrae in the lower back, called the **lumbar vertebrae**. They are the largest and strongest of all because they bear the weight of the entire upper body when you stand.

After the lumbar vertebrae comes a bony structure called the **sacrum**. The sacrum is

The coccyx at the end of your spine gives you support when you sit.

made up of five separate vertebrae in children. By the time children become adults, however, these five have joined together to form a single bone.

The last four vertebrae at the end of your spine make up the **coccyx**. These four vertebrae also join together as you get older to form a solid bone. The coccyx gives you support when you sit.

The sacrum, the hipbones, and the coccyx all join together to form the **pelvis**. The pelvis supports the bottom of the spine.

13

What Is Scoliosis?

If you looked at a normal spine from the front or back, it would look perfectly straight. But in fact, it is not. Looking at a spine from the side, you would see that

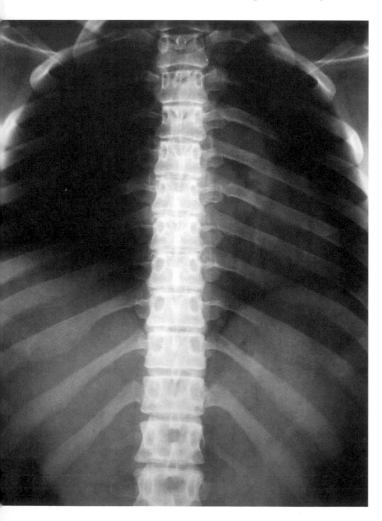

it is shaped like a long S that curves in a front-to-back direction. Take a look at a friend's back and you will notice how it curves back from the neck, over the upper part of the back, then swings in to the small of the back and out again.

In scoliosis the spine curves differently. It bends from side-to-side, in addition to the front-to-back curve. If it is a small curve, it may lean to one side, forming a C-shape. Large curves bend from one side to the other, forming an S.

This view of a spine from the front makes it look straight, although it really curves from front to back.

Most scoliosis cases are mild and just need to be checked over time. In these cases, the slight curve has no effect on how well the spine and back work. People with mild scoliosis can bend and turn without any problems, and they look and feel fine. In some cases, however, if scoliosis is not treated, the curve may **progress**, or get larger. As the curve increases, some of the vertebrae **rotate**, or turn. When this happens, the curve pushes parts of the body into unnatural positions. Then the back muscles have to work harder to keep the person standing up straight. It also puts unusual pressures on the disks between the vertebrae. They get worn and thin and don't cushion as well as they should. These effects can lead to backaches and pains.

The spine of a scoliosis patient curves from side to side.

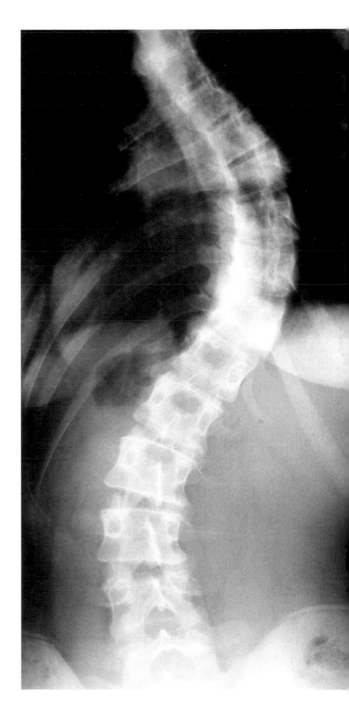

Activity 1: How Big Is the Curve?

If the curve in the spine gets very large, the length of the chest area gets shorter. You can see this for yourself if you cut off a 12-inch (30-centimeter) length of string. Lay it down on the table and make a curve in the middle. Now using a ruler, measure the distance from one end to the other. You will find that it is several inches shorter. The larger the curve, the more length it loses. Check that out with the string and ruler.

Large curves can cause big problems. There is much less room inside a shorter chest, and the heart and lungs are crowded together. It becomes harder to breathe, and the heart may have trouble working too. Fortunately, severe problems like these are not common.

Scoliosis can affect anyone — kids, teens, and adults. But it is most commonly seen in 10- to 13-year-olds. This is a time when children go through **growth spurts**, and may grow several inches within a single year. Scoliosis can occur in both boys and girls, but it is much more common in girls. Children are more likely to develop scoliosis if one of their parents, grandparents, aunts, uncles, brothers, or sisters has it.

Bad posture cannot cause scoliosis.

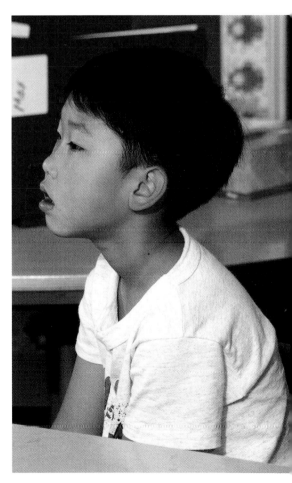

Scoliosis is not caused by bad **posture** or carrying a heavy bookbag. In fact, the opposite may happen — scoliosis may *cause* bad posture. But in most cases—about 80%—doctors do not know what causes the curving to occur. The most common form of scoliosis is **idiopathic scoliosis**. "Idiopathic" means that the cause is unknown. Most of the other 20% of scoliosis cases are caused by an injury or an illness. An injury to the back or even to the brain, which helps to control the muscles, can also lead to scoliosis. Some muscle diseases can also cause the spine to curve. Scoliosis may also develop in a person who has one leg that is shorter than the other.

A Heavy Load

Have you ever swung a heavy bookbag or backpack over one of your shoulders, and by the time you got home from school, your back and shoulders hurt? Many kids carry around as much as 20 pounds (9 kilograms) every single day. That's an awful lot of **strain** to put on your shoulder and back

Heavy bookbags can make your back hurt, but they cannot cause scoliosis.

muscles. And even though carrying around a heavy bookbag may not actually cause scoliosis, it can make you look like you have it. When you put an extra load on one shoulder, you tend to push against the weight. If you do that a lot, it may become a habit. So even when you are not carrying the load, that shoulder may look higher than the other, or it may lean forward.

These days, more and more kids are using backpacks on wheels. They roll their backpacks where they want to go. But some schools have rules against using backpacks on wheels. If you have to carry around a heavy bookbag, there are still some things you can do to avoid getting back and shoulder problems. For example, carrying a backpack over both shoulders will keep the shoulders balanced and lessen the amount of pressure on the back muscles. Or, if you carry a bookbag with a single strap, you could drape it over one shoulder and across your body. That way the weight isn't placed on just one side.

Some babies are born with scoliosis. These babies and other young children that develop scoliosis before the age of three usually get better on their own, without any treatment. This kind of scoliosis is rather rare, and it usually happens in boys. Scoliosis is more serious when it begins between the ages of four and ten. The curve may progress very quickly. Scoliosis most commonly develops between the ages of ten and thirteen. Sometimes the condition is first noticed in adults, but most likely it actually started during the early teen years. Once a person has stopped growing, the curve does not usually get worse. But it can still cause backaches and other problems.

Scoliosis is more serious in children age four and older.

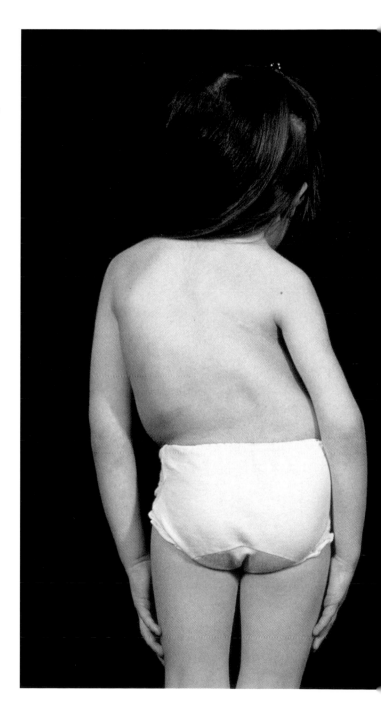

19

Other Curving Conditions

Scoliosis is not the only condition that involves a curving of the spine. Quasimodo, the Hunchback of Notre Dame, is a famous example of a fictional character with a condition called **kyphosis**, a severe backward bulging of the upper part of the spine. Kyphosis is sometimes called "roundback" because the whole upper back is rounded into a sort of hump.

Lordosis, or "swayback," is a condition that develops in the lower part of the spine. Looked at from the side, the spine is severely curved forward in the lumbar area, making the belly stick out.

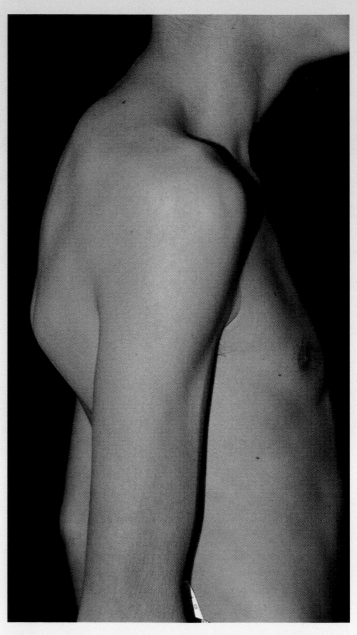

The person in this photo has kyphosis.

Spotting Scoliosis

It's not easy to spot signs of scoliosis. It's not like having a cold, when you may have a sore throat, runny nose, and a cough. Many people with scoliosis do not have any pain, and the condition can go unnoticed. But scoliosis does have characteristic signs that can be picked up during routine screening, either at school or at the doctor's office during regular check-ups.

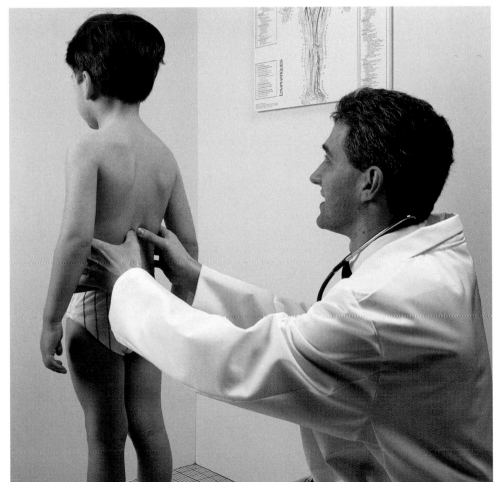

Many children undergo routine scoliosis screenings at a doctor's office or in school.

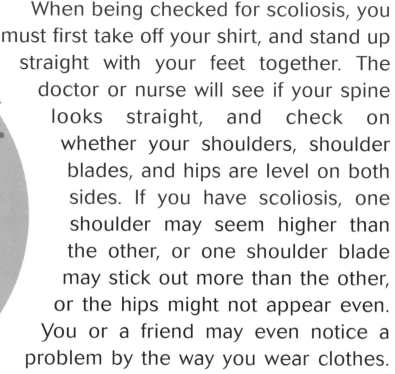

Did You Know....

If a child or teenager is found to have scoliosis, then the doctor will check any brothers or sisters since it runs in families.

When being checked for scoliosis, you must first take off your shirt, and stand up straight with your feet together. The doctor or nurse will see if your spine looks straight, and check on whether your shoulders, shoulder blades, and hips are level on both sides. If you have scoliosis, one shoulder may seem higher than the other, or one shoulder blade may stick out more than the other, or the hips might not appear even. You or a friend may even notice a problem by the way you wear clothes. For example, a shirt may be tight around one shoulder and loose around the other, or a skirt may look crooked.

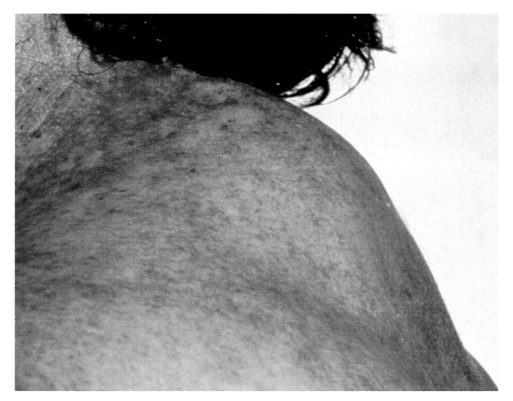

A hump on a person's back is one of the most obvious signs of scoliosis.

Next is the forward bending test. This test is commonly used in screening programs in schools. During this part of the exam, you have to bend forward at the waist with your knees straight and feet together. Bending forward will show if both sides of your upper and lower back are level and if your hips are level and even. One of the most obvious signs of scoliosis is a **rib hump**. This is caused when the rotating vertebrae (attached to the ribs) stick out more on one side of the back, producing a "hump."

If there are signs of scoliosis, you should see an **orthopedist**. This is a doctor who specializes in diseases and injuries involving bones and joints. The orthopedist will need to take **X-rays** of the spine to see the shape of the curve and how serious it is. He or she will measure the amount of curving on the X-ray film. This value is known as the **Cobb angle**, which is measured in degrees. If you have an S-curve, both curves have to be measured. Many health experts say that slight curves—between 10 and 15 degrees—do not need treatment, but should be

Did You Know...

Some of the most obvious signs of scoliosis are caused by the rotating vertebrae, rather than the curve itself.

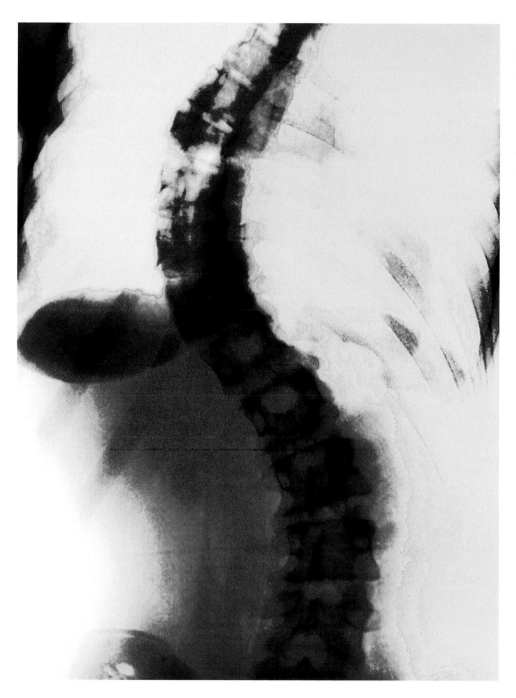

By taking an x-ray of the spine, an orthopedist can measure how severe a person's scoliosis has become.

Looks May Be Deceiving

C-shaped curves tend to be more noticeable in patients than S-shaped curves. For example, if you have a very large C-shaped curve in the thoracic vertebrae, the signs would be obvious: uneven shoulders and/or hips, and a rib hump. But if you have an S-shaped spine, with a large curve to the right in the thoracic vertebrae and just as much curving to the left in the lumbar vertebrae, your back may look normal. The double curve makes the back seem balanced. This kind of curve is harder to detect.

checked regularly in case the curve progresses. If the curve measures between 20 and 40 degrees, then you will have to wear a special back brace. But if the curve is over 40 degrees, surgery will be needed to correct the curve.

In most parts of the country, there are screening programs for scoliosis in schools. When scoliosis is identified and treated early, there is a good chance of keeping the curve from progressing. So, you would be less likely to need surgery.

Treating Scoliosis

If you had scoliosis 500 years ago, your treatment would have seemed like torture. The doctor would have strapped you to a rack and pulled your arms and legs in opposite directions in hopes of straightening out your spine. This kind of tug-of-war between body parts would go on for hours at a time over several months. Fortunately, doctors know much more about scoliosis now, and we have less painful and more effective methods of treatment.

A doctor explains a spinal x-ray to a young patient and her parents.

Although treatment is not usually necessary in cases where the scoliosis curve is less than 20 degrees, the condition will have to be watched carefully. The doctor will want to take X-rays every 3 to 6 months to see if the curve has progressed. If it has, treatment will probably be needed. For example, if the curve increases to 25 degrees in just a few months, you may need to wear an **orthopedic** back brace.

A brace acts as a holding device. Its job is to keep the spine from developing a larger curve. Pads placed

This scoliosis patient is being fitted for a brace.

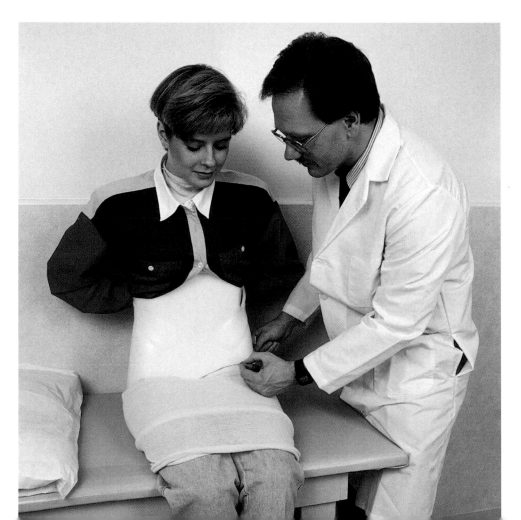

inside the brace push against the top of the spinal curve. The brace is worn for most of the day and night, so the steady pressure pushes the spine into a straighter position. Patients need to be checked regularly to make sure the brace is doing its job. You will also need to be fitted for new braces as you grow and develop.

You will need to wear the brace until you stop growing. If the curve was not too big to start with, it is not likely to get worse once you've reached your adult height. But if the curve is more than 50 degrees, it may continue to progress even after you have stopped growing. Surgery will probably be needed in these cases.

Did You Know...

The curve may straighten out a bit during brace treatment, but it's only temporary. After the brace is taken off, the curve will gradually go back to the way it was.

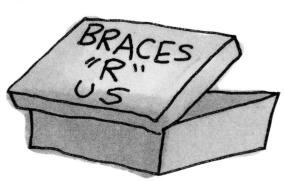

The brace most commonly used to treat scoliosis is the thoracic-lumbar-sacral-orthosis (TLSO), which is specially molded to the individual. *Orthosis* comes from a Greek word meaning "straight." The TLSO is a popular choice because it fits under the arms and can

A TLSO brace is commonly used to treat scoliosis.

be worn underneath clothes. This kind of brace comes in various forms, including the New York, Wilmington, Boston, and Miami braces, named after the cities where they were developed. Each type is a little different, but they all work in much the same way.

Most kids have to wear a brace for 18 to 20 hours a day. They are allowed to take it off for short periods of time for activities and bathing. The brace may feel very uncomfortable at first. Some people complain that it is difficult to move around or that they have a little trouble breathing, eating, and sometimes sleeping. Eventually, they get used to the brace and most of the problems go away.

The Charleston brace is a fairly new kind of brace being used to treat scoliosis. This brace bends the spine in the direction opposite to the curve, straightening it as much as possible. The Charleston brace puts a person's body in a really awkward position, making it hard to walk or do most activities. It can be worn only while sleeping.

A Milwaukee brace attaches at the neck and hips.

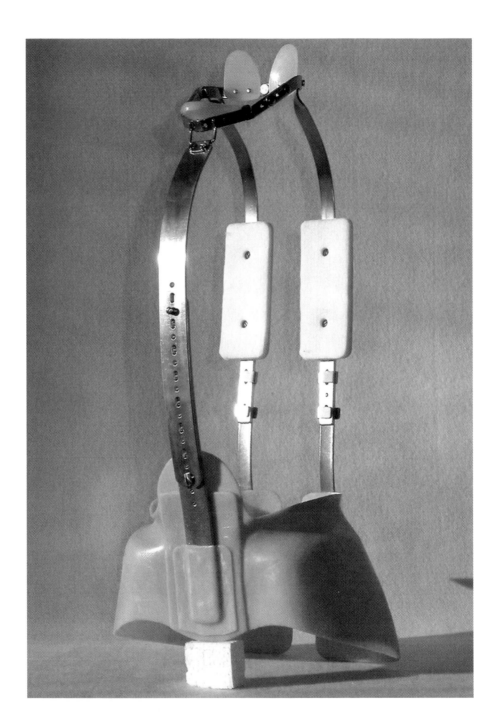

The oldest of all orthopedic braces for scoliosis is the Milwaukee brace. It is by far the least favorite brace among children and teenagers. That's because the Milwaukee brace consists of a plastic piece that wraps around the hips, a neck ring that keeps the head centered, and two rods that join these two parts and keep them in place. The neck ring makes it impossible to hide the brace under clothing, and kids might not like the way they look. Although this is the most effective type, what good is a brace if kids refuse to wear it? So, the Milwaukee brace is not commonly used to treat scoliosis anymore.

Many doctors suggest exercise for patients with scoliosis. However it is not considered a form of treatment because it does *not* stop scoliosis from progressing. Exercise does help, though, by strengthening back muscles, and it can ease the

The Brace Depends on the Place

A Milwaukee brace is recommended for scoliosis cases that involve a curve that is located higher than the sixth or seventh thoracic vertebrae. TLSO braces do not work on such high curves.

THE MILWAUKEE

YOU MUST BE THIS HIGH TO USE THIS BRACE

back pain that scoliosis sometimes causes. It is very important to keep the back muscles and surrounding tissues around the curve strong and healthy to give the spine the support it needs. Patients find that exercise helps their bodies move and bend more easily.

Severe cases of scoliosis need to be corrected with an operation known as **spinal fusion**. Spinal fusion may be suggested for cases where bracing is not helping to keep the curve from progressing, or if a curve is more than 40 degrees and continues to get worse. The idea is to join (fuse) some of the individual vertebrae into a solid bone so that the curve cannot progress. During the operation, the orthopedic surgeon removes small pieces of bone from the pelvis and puts them in between the vertebrae in the spine. The surgeon may also put in a metal rod to straighten out the curve. Screws and hooks are used to fuse the rod to the vertebrae to keep the spine straight until the pieces of bone join together. The rod is usually left in the back even after the bones are fused together because it isn't harmful and removing it would involve another operation. Surgery will not make a spinal curve completely straight, but it will help correct it by as much as 50%. This means that if you have a 65-degree curve, it may be reduced to about 30 to 35 degrees after surgery.

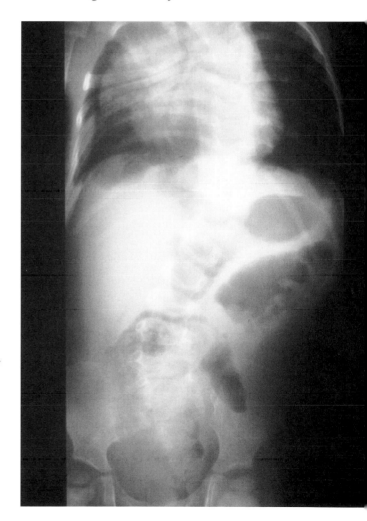

Severe scoliosis cases are usually treated with surgery.

Living With Scoliosis

You've been told you have scoliosis, and now you have to wear a brace. The brace feels uncomfortable, and some of your clothes don't fit over it. You look at yourself in the mirror and aren't too happy with the way you look.

If you have scoliosis, you need to make a lot of changes from the way you did things before. You can't do everything you used to do. Tasks that used to be simple — such as tying your shoes or even going to the bathroom—are now more difficult. But eventually you will learn new ways to do things. In fact, doctors believe that kids should continue doing their everyday activities, including taking gym class in school. If it

Scoliosis patients should continue with their regular activities, including gym class.

becomes too difficult to play sports or other physical activities with your brace on, you can take it off for a short period of time. Your daily routine should also include exercises that strengthen your back muscles and keep you physically fit.

You'll also need to learn some tricks to keep your brace from causing problems. For example, the heat and sweat that build up in the brace may cause skin problems, especially during the summer months. Your skin may become red and itchy. But wearing a T-shirt

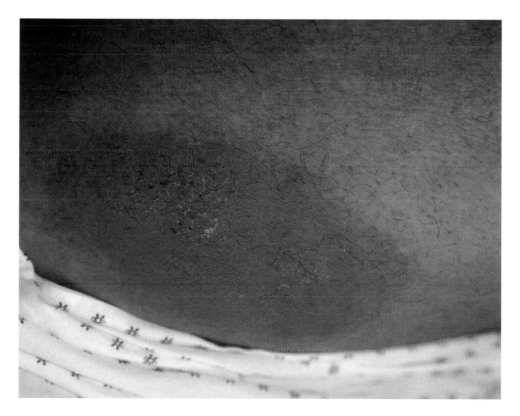

Sometimes a brace will rub against a patient's skin and cause a rash.

or a body stocking underneath the brace keeps it from rubbing against your skin. Washing every day and putting powder on areas under the brace keep the skin clean and dry and help prevent rashes.

While you are trying to get used to all these changes in your life, you may be afraid that other kids won't understand, and that they will treat you differently. Some kids may tease you and make you feel bad about the way you look. And that can really hurt your **self-esteem**. Kids with scoliosis sometimes feel bad about themselves, but this doesn't have to happen. Some friends will be really nice and go out of their way to help. Parents and other family members can provide a lot of love and support too. When you are surrounded by people who care about you and understand your condition, it can give you the confidence you need to feel good about yourself. Remember, although the brace may be awkward to live with now, it will make you stronger and healthier in the future.

Activity 2: Develop Good Posture

How many times have you heard, "Sit up straight!" Although poor posture doesn't give you scoliosis, it can make you look bad.

Normally, the muscles in the back, neck, and shoulders keep your spine straight. Even though it sometimes seems hard to keep your back straight while sitting or standing, you actually use more muscles when you slouch.

Do you have good posture? Good posture means that your shoulders do not hunch or droop, and your lower back does not lean inward. Many people don't even realize when they are slouching. In this activity, let's find out how many times a day you catch yourself slouching. For one day, from the time you wake up until you go to bed, pay attention to how you stand and sit. Write down every time you slouch, then try to straighten up. At the end of the day, check out the results.

If your posture isn't as good as you thought it was, try this exercise. Stand with your back against the wall with your knees bent and your heels about 9 inches (23 centimeters) away from the wall. Now keeping your head against the wall, flatten your back as much as you can, and slowly straighten your legs to push upward.

Glossary

cartilage—rubbery material at the end of bones

cervical vertebrae—the top seven vertebrae in the neck

Cobb angle—the distance, measured in degrees, between the curves in the spine of a scoliosis patient

disk—small circles of rubbery cartilage that act as cushions between the vertebrae

growth spurt—a fairly short period of time in which a young person grows noticeably taller

coccyx—the last four vertebrae at the end of the spine that join together to form the "tailbone"

idiopathic scoliosis—a sideways curvature of the spine, the cause of which is unknown

joints—connections between bones, such as elbows and knees

kyphosis—severe curving of the upper part of the spine. This condition is also called "roundback" because the whole upper back is rounded into a sort of "hump."

ligaments—tough bands of tissue connecting bones

lordosis—severe curving of the lower part of the spine. This condition is also called "swayback" because the lower back is curved forward.

lumbar vertebrae—the first five vertebrae after the thoracic vertebrae located in the lower back

muscles—strong, elastic tissues that pull on bones or other structures and move body parts

orthopedic—something that works to correct or prevent problems with the spine

orthopedist—a doctor who specializes in diseases and injuries involving the bones and joints

pelvis—the structure formed by the sacrum, the hipbones, and the coccyx

posture—the way people hold their backs and shoulders when they walk and sit. Good posture includes keeping the back straight and the shoulders back.

progress (pronounced pro-GRESS)—to worsen

rib hump—a sign of scoliosis that occurs when rotating vertebrae (attached to the ribs) stick out more on one side of the back, producing a "hump"

rotate—to turn around a center point

sacrum—the second five lumbar vertebrae in the hip area; in adults, they are usually joined together into a single bone

scoliosis—a sideways curving of the spine

self-esteem—feeling good about yourself

spinal fusion—an operation designed to join some of the individual vertebrae into solid bone so that the scoliosis curve cannot progress

spine—the backbone; the central support of the skeleton, made up of individual bones called vertebrae

strain—to injure by overuse or by exerting too much pressure

thoracic vertebrae—the twelve middle vertebrae located in the upper back; they are attached to the ribs

vertebrae (singular **vertebra**)—the individual bones of the spine

X-ray—a special way to photograph the insides of something solid

Learning More

Books

Llamas, Andreu. *Muscles and Bones*. Milwaukee, WI: Gareth Stevens, 1998.

Llewellen, Claire. *The Big Book of Bones*. New York: Peter Bedrick Books, 1998.

Lyons, Brooke et al. *Scoliosis: Ascending the Curve*. New York: M. Evans and Company, Inc., 1999.

Neuwirth, Michael and Kevin Osborn. *The Scoliosis Sourcebook*. New York: Contemporary Books, 2001.

Schommer, Nancy. *Stopping Scoliosis*. Garden City Park, NY: Avery Publishing Group Inc., 1991.

Silverstein, Alvin. *The Skeletal System*. Brookfield, CT: Twenty-First Century Books, 1995.

Taylor, Barbara. *Skeletons*. New York: DK Publishing, 1998.

Getting Things Straight: A Guide to Scoliosis
http://www.kidshealth.org/teen/health_problems/diseases/scoliosis_prt.htm
This site, provided by kidshealth.org, has general information about scoliosis, including diagnosis, treatment, and dealing with the condition.

National Scoliosis Foundation, Inc.
5 Cabot Place
Stoughton, MA 02072
(800) 673-6922
(617) 341-6333
http://www.scoliosis.org

Q and A About Scoliosis in Children and Adolescents
http:www.nih.gov/niams/healthinfo/scochild.htm
This site is provided by the National Institute of Arthritis and Musculoskeletal and Skin Diseases, which is a part of the National Institutes of Health (NIH). This is a fact sheet that gives an overview of scoliosis including a description of the condition, who gets it, diagnosis, and treatment.

The Scoliosis Association, Inc.
P.O. Box 811705
Boca Raton, FL 33481-1705
(800) 800-0669
http://www.scoliosis-assoc.org

Scoliosis Can Be Treated

http://kidshealth.org/kid/health_problems/bone/scolio.html
This kid-friendly site gives general information about scoliosis, including what it is, testing for it, and how it's treated.

Scoliosis: Keri's Story

http://kidshealth.org/teen/health_problems/personal_stories/scoliosis_keri.html
This kidshealth.org site gives one girl's personal story of what happened when she found out she had scoliosis.

Scoliosis Research Society

6300 N. River Road
Suite 727
Rosemont, IL 60018-4226
(847) 698-1627
http://www.srs.org

Index

About the Authors

Dr. Alvin Silverstein is a professor of biology at the College of Staten Island of the City University of New York. **Virginia B. Silverstein** is a translator of Russian scientific literature. The Silversteins first worked together on a research project at the University of Pennsylvania. Since then, they have produced 6 children and more than 180 published books for young people.

Laura Silverstein Nunn, a graduate of Kean College, has been helping with her parents' books since her high-school days. She is the coauthor of more than 50 books on diseases and health, science concepts, endangered species, and pets. Laura lives with her husband Matt and their young son Cory in a rural New Jersey town not far from her childhood home.